CRYING IS MY SEASON

a small book about big feelings

Melissa Marie Bowers

Crying Is My Season
A Small Book About Big Feelings
Written by Melissa Marie Bowers

ISBN: 979-8-9946948-0-0 (Paperback)

Published by: Independently Published

Printed in the United States of America
First Edition, 2026

Contains brief quoted material from The Little Prince by Antoine de Saint-Exupéry, used with attribution for illustrative purposes. Includes attributed quotation from Isak Dinesen: "The cure for anything is salt water: sweat, tears, or the sea."

Publisher's Note:
This is a work of creative nonfiction. Certain names, identifying details, and experiences may have been changed to protect the privacy of individuals.

“For I know the plans I have for you,” declares the Lord,
“plans to prosper you and not to harm you,
plans to give you hope and a future.”

— Jeremiah 29:11 (NIV)

DEDICATION

To those who pour into me with love, patience, prayer, and presence – and to my one true Lord and Savior, Jesus Christ, who carries me when I cannot walk myself. He who reads my tears as prayers when my words and thoughts fall silent.

A WORD FROM A FRIEND

"I just read your story, and now I am in tears! It is beautiful—simple yet complex, sweet and honest, evocative and poignant. So many words come to my mind. What it isn't is bitter, angry, or painful, but rather joyful and reflective of this season, despite its challenges and its tears.

I've always loved the saying by Isak Dinesen: 'The cure for anything is salt water—sweat, tears, or the sea.' One of my favorite all-time books is The Little Prince by Antoine de Saint-Exupéry. There is a quote from the book I love so much: 'C'est tellement mystérieux, le pays de larmes.' It means, 'The land of tears is so mysterious.'

I cry easily and often, and others don't always know how to handle it, but they are essential for my being—and all beings. I love the center of the book where you describe tears as 'salty information pathways' and as part of your internal weather pattern; that they show strength and not weakness, joy as well as grief; and that you do not apologize for them (why do we do that, anyway?).

I love it, and I love you, and I stand in awe of your clarity and willingness to share it. Well done, my sweet friend!"

— Anne Brown

Some seasons are loud.
This one is quiet.

This is the season where tears come
without warning,

without invitation.

They arrive at dawn, as a blessing at sunrise,

In the kitchen, *without cutting onions* --

And in the middle of a perfectly ordinary day.

Sometimes when I am alone.

Other times when I am held
by someone who loves me.

The script changed without warning.

There were words I didn't want to learn.

Beautiful moments I was preparing for,
even as I tried to slow their arrival.

My children became adults --

adventuring, discovering,
carrying their courage
far from home.

I carry pride …

and uncertainty
in the same breath.

I received news.

Tests I didn't want to complete ... *and that I couldn't study for.*

Treatments I didn't ask for.

Some days I am brave.
Some days I am numb.

Every day,
I am hopeful.

Tears are not a sign of weakness.

They are streams of salty information pathways.

They tell me I'm alive.
They show me I care.

I stopped apologizing for them.

They fall like rain --
part of my weather system.

In fact, they have weather patterns of their own --

-- sometimes light and misty, sometimes hard and torrential,

often steady, a constant flow.

And still,
today keeps showing up.

The sunrise doesn't cancel
because I am in "*season.*"

The sparkles in my morning glass of water still dance,

still rise to the surface --

just as I do.

I hold the celebration of this season in my heart
while calming racing thoughts in my mind.

I can hold grief in one hand
and gratitude in the other.

This season won't last forever,
but while it is here,

I will let it move at its own pace.

I celebrate today --

with its laughter, with its tears,
its hope, and its *joy.*

Because crying is not the opposite of joy.

It is one of the ways joy makes room for *itself*.

this is not the end.

www.ingramcontent.com/pod-product-compliance
Lightning Source LLC
LaVergne TN
LVHW070224110826
845147LV00003B/643

* 9 7 9 8 9 9 4 6 9 4 8 0 0 *